The

Conversation

Piece

2

By **Bret Nicholaus** and **Paul Lowrie**

The Conversation Piece

The Christmas Conversation Piece

The Mom and Dad Conversation Piece

Think Twice!

Toe Tappin' Trivia

The Talk of the Tee

Have You Ever . . .

The Check Book

Who We Are

The Conversation Piece 2

The Tattletale Game

The Christmas Letters

The Conversation Piece 2

[A New Generation of Questions]

**Bret Nicholaus
and Paul Lowrie
The Question Guys™**

Ballantine Books • New York

A Ballantine Book

The Ballantine Publishing Group

Copyright © 2000 by **Bret Nicholaus** and **Paul Lowrie**

Illustrations copyright © 2000 by Randy Bray

All rights reserved under International and Pan-American Copyright

Conventions. Published in the United States by The Ballantine Publishing

Group, a division of Random House, Inc., New York, and simultaneously in

Canada by Random House of Canada Limited, Toronto.

Ballantine and colophon are registered trademarks of Random House, Inc.

www.randomhouse.com/BB/

Library of Congress Catalog Card Number: 96-096298

Manufactured in the United States of America

First Edition: October 2000

10 9 8 7 6 5 4 3 2 1

Acknowledgments

Bret and Paul wish to sincerely thank everyone—family, friends, and customers—who have supported their efforts and books along the way.

II Corinthians 4:6–10

Welcome

Even without an official introduction, it probably wouldn't take you but a few seconds to figure out how to use this book. It's not a lengthy treatise on ways to reduce your taxes, increase your investments, or stabilize your metabolism; it is, quite simply, a collection of approximately 300 original questions that foster fun and thought-provoking conversations. To put it another way, it's a tool you can use to take your talks to another level.

Just like our original work, *The Conversation Piece*, the questions in this exciting sequel are appropriate for both adults *and* children; you will find nothing offensive or controversial anywhere in this book. Indeed, the primary goal of *The Conversation Piece 2* is the same as that of the other books we've written: to provide people of all ages with questions that encourage positive, entertaining conversations and creative thinking.

For those of you who have bought any of our conversation-themed books in the past, we want to take this opportunity to sincerely thank you. For those who are buying one of our titles for the first time, we would like to welcome you to the "Conversation Piece Club"; if you're like millions of other people, you'll be hooked on the art of asking questions in no time. We hope that you thoroughly enjoy the ensuing conversations and learn more about yourself, your family, and your friends than you ever thought possible. Allow yourself to dream big and your discussions are sure to take off in exciting directions that you never knew existed.

Our biggest wish for each of you is this: May every question lead to a great conversation, may every conversation lead to a new insight, and may every new insight remind you that the answers to life are found in the questions we ask.

Bret Nicholaus and **Paul Lowrie**,
The Question Guys™

There are countless opportunities and places for this book to be enjoyed. A few of them are listed below:

Dinner Parties

Family Gatherings

**New Groups
(as icebreaker
questions)**

Car Trips

Dates

**Personal
Reflection**

Table Topics

Brainstorming
Sessions

School
Classrooms

Creative
Writing

Job
Interviews

Stocking
Stuffers

Hostess Gifts

The

Conversation

Piece

2

If your life were a weather vane, in which direction would it be pointed right now?

2

If, like milk or the newspaper, you could have anything of your choice delivered to your doorstep every morning, what particular item would you want it to be?

3

Thinking back to all the great TV series finales that you've seen over the years, which show do you believe had the best final episode?

4

Which month of the year do you think would best describe your personality?

5

If you could have the voice of any famous person, living or deceased, whose voice would you want to claim as your own?

6

In your opinion, what is the single most significant event that has occurred in world history during the last thousand years? (Define "significant" however you wish.)

7

If you could have a grand, beautiful front porch with a relaxing porch swing overlooking any place or thing in the world, what would it overlook?

8

What is one vacation destination that many people think is just fabulous, but which you personally have no desire to ever visit (or revisit)?

9

If the decision were up to you, exactly how much taller or shorter than you actually are would you like to be?

10

Of all the great success stories that you've heard or read about, which one do you find the most inspiring?

11

If you could change or add *one* detail to any famous painting or other work of art, which piece of art would you pick and what would the change be?

1 2

If you were five years younger but knew everything at that age that you've actually learned over the last five years, what is one thing that you would definitely do differently than you did?

1 3

You've no doubt heard the expression "Wake up and smell the coffee!" If you could wake up every morning to the distinct smell of any one thing except coffee, what would you choose?

Suppose that we still lived in an age when kings and queens ruled the lands. If you were crowned an absolute monarch, what is the very first rule or law you would impose on your kingdom?

The year is 1850, and a town is springing up in California as a result of the Gold Rush. Because you were the first prospector to arrive in the area, you've been asked to name the new town. What would you name it?

16

Suppose that right now you could be at your favorite vacation spot, reading your favorite book, listening to your favorite CD, and eating your favorite food. What would be your choices for those four categories?

17

If you could take a ride on anything in the world, what would you most want to ride?

18

If you could add one very unusual feature to the inside of your home (e.g., a waterfall in the living room), what would it be?

19

What is one major problem, either in our own nation or throughout the world, that you honestly feel we will have pretty well solved within twenty-five years?

20

If you could fall in love with someone in any city in the world, what city would you choose?

21

If you had to come up with one question for a national opinion poll, what question would you most want to pose to the American public?

If you had
to write
a one-sentence
mission statement
for your life,
what would
it be?

23

"If I had a dollar for every time I
_____, I'd be a rich
person." How would you fill in the blank?

24

The swish of a three-point shot, the
crack of a bat hitting a home run ball,
the crunch of helmet meeting helmet . . .
In your opinion, what is the greatest sound
in all of sports?

Suppose that you could buy stock in famous individuals rather than in companies. In what particular person would you be the most willing to invest a portion of your money? (Just as with a company's stock, consider the *future* potential of the person in which you are investing.)

What is your favorite food that begins with the letter C?

If you were a professional athlete, what number would you want to wear on your uniform?

Imagine that you wake up one morning and are handed five hundred dollars . . . and told that you must have it spent by midnight of that same day. You are also told that any tangible objects you buy, unless they are completely used up, will have to be given back at the stroke of midnight. How would you quickly and enjoyably spend this large amount of cash?

Suppose that everywhere you went you had to carry a shoe box around with you, and in that box you had to keep what you consider to be the most unusual or unique object you own. When people invariably ask you to show them what's in the box, what item would be revealed?

Babe Ruth, James Dean, Elvis Presley . . . If you could bring back one deceased superstar for one final performance in their respective field, whom would you choose?

Considering all of the Walt Disney Company's animated films, which animated character remains your all-time favorite?

If you could somehow see yourself as you will look physically ten years from now, how do you suppose you will look? (Be as specific as you can.)

If you had to write a brief message on a dollar bill that many people would eventually see as the currency circulates, what message would you write?

If you were in charge of determining which U.S. president's face would appear on the front of a brand-new coin, which former chief executive would receive the honor?

If you could create a brand-new
instrument, how would it look and how
would it sound?

If you could reverse or rearrange the order
of anything at all (e.g., the four seasons),
what would you choose?

37

If you could own a home on the shore of any body of water in the world, which waterfront would you choose?

38

What movie that you have watched most closely parallels your own life to this point?

39

Considering all the big-screen movies that you've ever seen, which one do you believe has had the greatest emotional impact on you?

40

If you were going to start your own book publishing company, what would you name it?

Which punctuation mark would best describe your personality?

You are in charge of creating a beautiful garden for a large estate, but you have been asked to plant only three types of flowers in that garden. Which three kinds of flowers would you cultivate?

If you were in charge of coming up with a new movie rating for the motion picture industry (in addition to the existing ratings like G, PG, PG-13, R, etc.), what would the new rating be?

In your opinion, what is the most adorable-looking baby animal?

Suppose that you had the opportunity to choose three people with whom to eat dinner: a famous sports figure, a movie star, and a popular singer. Who are the three people that would be joining you at the table?

You've been asked to create a brand-new road sign that will be put up, where appropriate, on streets throughout your town. People in your town will be expected to obey it just as they would any other road sign. What will your new sign command drivers to do?

47

If you could permanently rid the world of any one insect or other creepy-crawly thing, which one would it be?

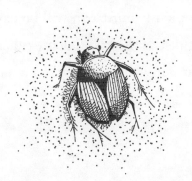

48

What serves as the greatest motivation for you in your daily life?

49

Old-fashioned gaslights, wrought-iron fences, fountains . . . If you were designing a town square for a growing community, what unique features would you be sure to give it?

50

What is one food you truly disliked at one time but that you have grown to enjoy?

51

Just thinking about it will probably make you want to sing it: What is your all-time-favorite theme song from a TV show?

52

What is the quaintest small town you've ever had the pleasure of visiting?

53

If you could swallow a pill that would stop anything of your choice from ever happening to you again, what would the pill permanently end?

If you were a member of a renowned musical association whose job it was to determine the singer with the best voice in the history of music, which singer would get your vote?

Going to the dentist, filing your income taxes, being summoned for jury duty . . . What activity that you *have* to do every once in a while do you dread the most?

If you could take any animal native to a continent other than our own and introduce it into the wild of our *own* country, what animal would you choose? (Assume that the animal would somehow be able to survive in our part of the world.)

If you could renovate and/or revitalize any city in America, presumably one that is currently depressed, which one would you choose?

If people could truly read your mind, what would they discover that you think about most often?

59

If you were a multimillionaire, what do you believe you would be doing at this very moment?

60

If you could investigate any famous archives, which one would you choose?

61

If you could be the editor of any magazine in circulation, having significant input as to the style and content of the publication, which magazine would you choose?

62

If you could have a cookie-jar-size container full of anything you wanted—anything but cookies or money—with what would you want the jar to be filled?

63

When people find out what you do for a living, what is the most typical question that they are likely to ask you regarding your job?

64

Jack Nicklaus, Muhammad Ali, Michael Jordan . . . In your opinion, who was the greatest sports star of the twentieth century?

65

If ten people who know you were asked to write down on a piece of paper the one adjective that each of them thinks best describes you, what do you think would be the most common word written?

What is the most incredible weather
event you've ever been through?

In the classroom of life, what lesson do
you believe we must continuously try to
master day after day?

68

If you could live in any state other than the one in which you currently reside, which state would you choose?

69

If you could make one request of all people everywhere, what would you ask that they do (or not do)?

70

In your opinion, what is the most fascinating object in the sky?

If you had been a youth growing up in the 1800s, who do you think your hero would have been?

Suppose that every night for one full year, your dinner had to consist of the cuisine from a foreign country—the same foreign country each night for a year. Which country's food would you choose?

73

If you could be any type of bird in the world, what bird would you be?

74

What is one annual event that, if you miss it, leaves you feeling like your year is somehow incomplete?

If you could create a drive-through that would offer one product or service while you waited in your vehicle, what type of drive-through would you want to create?

Generally speaking, which holiday on the calendar do you feel is most neglected by people?

77

What is the most boring speech you've ever heard in person?

78

If you could be any famous person's therapist, whose would you be?

79

Doctors tell us that we should drink at least eight glasses of water per day. If drinking eight daily glasses of any other liquid could keep you just as healthy, what would you be drinking?

If you could have any round object in the world, what spherical item would you want?

81

Picture yourself standing in a town about a hundred and fifty years ago. What are five scents that you would expect to smell as you walk through the town?

82

If you could create the ultimate hotel, something as big and grand as those in Las Vegas or Disney World, what would your hotel look like upon completion?

Shaving, brushing your teeth, combing your hair . . . If you could permanently eliminate one morning activity that you must do on a daily basis, what would it be?

Forget about soft sounds like babbling brooks, gentle showers, and warbling birds; what is your favorite *loud* sound?

If you were left alone for one hour with nothing more than a pen and a notepad, what would you be inclined to write or draw during those sixty minutes?

If you could speed up anything, either in your personal life or in the world at large, what specifically would you want to go faster?

If you could witness anything at all in super-slow-motion, what would you want to see?

What is the most outrageous impersonation that you do when nobody is around (or, maybe, when people *are* around)?

If you had to live out in the country for the next couple of years, what particular aspect of your new environment do you think you would find the most satisfying?

Suppose that you are at a party where you meet an alert and astute hundred-year-old person. Since everyone wants to talk to this individual, you only have time to ask one question of him or her. What would you ask this centenarian?

91

If you were in charge of coming up with the name for a new NBA franchise in the city of Anchorage, Alaska, what would you name the team?

92

Aside from your family, friends, or pets, what would be the most difficult thing for you to give up in your life?

93

If you could see a breathtaking sunset anywhere in the world, where would you want it to be?

94

If, through the benefit of hindsight, you could go back in time to warn any famous person in history about something, whom would you visit and what would you tell that individual to help him or her avoid a tragic mistake or fate?

95

What is one field or profession that you never pursued, but that you think you probably would have been quite good at?

96

What is your favorite "big" word to pull out of your vocabulary when trying to impress people in conversations?

97

In one sentence, what do you believe is the secret of life?

98

If you could own any classic car, which one would you choose?

99

In your opinion, what was—or is—the most ridiculous-looking fashion trend of all time?

100

Suppose that a monument much like Mount Rushmore was being built to honor the four greatest Americans in history, sans presidents. Which four American faces would you recommend be carved into the stone?

101

If you could rekindle any long-lost childhood friendship, with whom would you reestablish ties?

What technological breakthrough or invention absolutely blows your mind when you stop and think about what it is actually capable of doing?

If there could be only one snowfall a year and you could determine the very day on which that snow would fall, what day would you choose? (Assume that Christmas Eve or Day is not an option.)

If you could introduce a new degree into the nation's colleges and universities, what degree would you choose?

105

What is the greatest distance you've ever driven in a single day?

106

If money could buy anything intangible (besides happiness), what would you be purchasing tomorrow?

If someone offered to give you a dozen of anything you wanted, what would you choose?

If you were given ten thousand dollars that had to be divided into three equal parts and then invested for ten years in the stock of three different companies, which three companies would you choose?

109

If you could step back in time to witness the construction of anything that was built prior to the year 1700, what would you want to see being built?

110

If you had to permanently eliminate one primary color from the spectrum, which one would you be willing to give up?

1 1 1

M ost of us do, or have done, something that other people would generally consider daring, dangerous, or even foolish. In what way have you most defiantly tempted fate during your life?

1 1 2

I f someone was looking for you in a bookstore, in which section would they be most likely to find you?

1 1 3

Over the last two hundred years or so, the world has certainly advanced and changed in unprecedented ways. Nonetheless, can you think of at least one aspect of life that has remained virtually unchanged throughout the last two centuries?

1 1 4

What is one item that you think will *never* become obsolete?

The geography in some states changes so dramatically from one part to the other that it almost seems like two states (consider the difference between eastern and western Colorado). If you could zone off a part of any one state, thus forming a new state, which state would you divide?

116

What is your all-time-favorite Academy Award–winning movie?

117

What do you forget to do more often than anything else?

118

What was your favorite thing to pretend when you were a young child?

On a scale of one to ten (with one being you can't stand it and ten being you love it), how well do you like your given first name?

Suppose that you were going to be embarking on a monthlong trek through the jungles of South America, hundreds of miles from civilization. You must choose four people to go along with you—one person from each of any four different professions—but they may only bring along as many of their respective "tools of the trade" as they can fit into their backpack. Given this information, what would the four people who accompany you do for their living?

What particular piece of personal information, when asked of you in general conversation, are you least likely to be completely truthful about?

You've no doubt heard the expression "It's a dog's life." In your opinion, what particular aspect of a dog's life seems the most enviable?

Imagine that you've been chosen to deliver a thirty-minute speech at a business reception to a group of a hundred people— all of whom are of the opposite sex. As you've been told to choose any topic you wish, what subject would you choose to entertain your audience?

As part of an assignment on the study of human behavior, you have been asked to do a couple of hours of plain and simple "people watching." Where do you think would be the best place to go and conduct this entertaining research?

Except professional sports or entertainment, what job looks like so much fun that you would be willing to do it even if it meant accepting a decrease in dollars from your current salary?

126

If you could combine the basic characteristics of any two sports to create a new sport, which two would you combine and how would the new game be played?

127

When it comes to television advertising, what brand do you think has the most creative commercials?

128

What is your biggest pet peeve?

129

If you had to single out one year in the history of our nation that you believe had the greatest impact on what we as a country have become, what year would get your vote?

130

If you could teach everyone in the world one skill, what would you teach them?

131

If, for one month, you had to live day and night in any one retail store, which one would it be?

132

If, for one year, you could live at any famous residence or home in the entire world, which one would you pick?

What is the most exquisite restaurant at which you've ever eaten?

While using the bathroom during someone's party, you notice that the host/hostess has accidentally left his/her checkbook lying on the sink. On a scale of one to ten (with one being not at all tempted and ten being extremely tempted), how tempted would you be to open the checkbook and investigate that person's spending habits?

135

"Money doesn't grow on trees," or so the expression goes. Imagine, however, that something unusual—besides money—*could* be grown on trees, available to be picked by you whenever the urge struck. What would you want your tree to produce?

136

If you had a good voice and had the opportunity to record a duet with any singer living today, whom would you choose as your partner?

137

What are your three favorite states to visit on a vacation?

138

If you were ranking the four seasons in the order of your favorite to your least favorite, how would the seasons be ranked?

139

If you could call anyone in the world for help in every difficult situation you encounter in life, whom would you call? (Assume that the person would always answer the phone.)

140

Suppose that you were entered in an amateur photography contest whose rules allowed you to shoot any object in the world, regardless of whether it is natural or man-made. What object would you photograph for the contest?

If you could have a penthouse view of the city skyline in any city of your choice, which city would you choose?

In your own not-so-humble opinion, what is your most likable quality?

143

If, for fun, you could fly in anything other than an airplane, what would you choose?

144

Suppose that a furniture company has offered to make you an armchair, but instead of covering it in standard leather, the chair will be covered in the rind or skin of a fruit. Assuming that the skin would always retain its fresh texture and color, what type of fruit skin do you think would make your armchair most a"peel"ing?

What is one thing that for years you've been saying you should do but as yet have not done?

Suppose that you are living in the year 1870 and, through the use of time travel, you are being thrust a hundred and fifty years into the future—to the year 2020. You are to take with you three objects of any size that will show these futuristic people what life is like in the 1800s (a good example of an object would be a covered wagon). What three objects would you take along with you?

147

Which popular sport above all others do you personally find the most boring?

148

If you had to give yourself a sobriquet, what would it be?

In hindsight, what particular class in school above all others do you wish you had paid more attention to or taken more seriously?

150

What wild animal do you think makes the most interesting sound?

151

If your taste buds could be altered so that the taste of any one food would be dramatically intensified whenever you ate it, which food would you choose?

152

Here's a question that makes good scents: What month of the year does your *nose* anticipate the most?

153

If someone put a world atlas in front of you for fifteen minutes, what part of the world would you be most likely to study?

Suppose that you were in a job interview and the interviewer said, "Give me one good reason why we should hire you." Assuming that the answer was meant to reflect the type of person you are rather than your technical skills, what would your response be?

155

If you were a songwriter drawing from recent experiences in your own life as material for your next big hit, what would be the song's title?

156

What is one product or item that you absolutely detest shopping for?

157

In what part of our country can you not even imagine having to live?

158

What is something you do that is in the opposite order of how most people do it? (Example: Reading the last page of a book first.)

You've been asked to complete a joke for the writers of *The Tonight Show*. The opening joke is designed to get the audience rolling, so you need to make it a good one. The joke begins, "It's been so hot in California this week that _____ _____." How would you finish it?

160

What is something you always used to love to do that during the last few years or so you feel like you've "outgrown" or simply lost interest in doing?

161

What do you consider to be the most beautiful foreign accent?

If you were
a fish, what
would a fisherman
want to use as
bait if he really
wanted to catch
you quickly?

163

If you were asked to create a brand-new board game that would be the hottest new rage at parties, what type of game would you invent?

164

What song has the power to bring you to tears faster than any other?

165

What is the strangest dream you can remember having?

166

If you could significantly change one physical characteristic of the earth's surface (e.g., 100,000-foot-tall mountains), what would it be?

167

What do you consider to be the quintessential sound of summer?

168

If you could bring to life any fictional character from any book, whom would you choose?

169

If an architect offered to build you a swimming pool in the shape of any state, which state would you choose?

170

If you could take any existing holiday and make it last two full days instead of one, which holiday and its respective traditions would you extend?

If your alarm clock could make any sound at all to wake you up in the morning, what sound would you want it to make?

172

Jackie Robinson, Amelia Earhart, John Glenn . . . If you could have experienced the thrill of being any famous "first" in history, what "first" would you want to be?

173

You've been offered the chance to print any message you want on a large billboard along the interstate, but the message can be no longer than ten words. What would your billboard proclaim?

174

If rain could fall in any scent, what scent would you want it to be?

If you had to spend one year researching and documenting the activities and lifestyle of any animal in the wild, which animal would you choose to observe?

If it were physically or geographically possible to move any famous European site or landmark to an area near you, what would you like to see relocated for your viewing pleasure?

Imagine an absolutely ideal setting that you could step into—utopia, if you will. This is meant to be a scene so perfect that you would never, ever want to leave it. How would you describe your ideal setting?

If you were asked to put something besides a star on top of a Christmas tree, something that significantly relates to who you are, what would adorn the top of the tree? (Example: If you love country music, a cowboy hat.)

179

In what aspect of your life do you feel you can honestly say that you've been very lucky?

180

If you could see the world, figuratively speaking, from someone else's point of view, whose view in particular would you like to see?

What is the best one hundred dollars you've ever spent?

What is the most awe-inspiring
Olympic moment that you've seen
during your lifetime?

If you could change one—and only one—
aspect of the U.S. presidential election
process, what would it be?

184

If you could work for any corporation in the world, which one would it be?

185

Who needs pictures! What is one memorable moment in your past that you can still see perfectly clearly in your mind's eye?

If you had to choose a job that generally requires that its employees wear a uniform (besides an athlete), what job would you choose?

Besides using this book, what is one way you can think of that would regularly make dinnertime more interesting or exciting?

188

If you could know without a shadow of a doubt the answer to one question that has always troubled you, what question would you want answered?

189

If you could have been born at any other time of the year than your true birth date, what date (month and day) would you have preferred most of all?

190

If you could have in your personal possession any one artifact from all of history, what object would you want to own?

191

What is one item beyond your wallet and keys that you never leave home without?

192

Barnum & Bailey's circus was once known as "The Greatest Show on Earth." If you were in charge of giving that same title to something incredibly entertaining in this day and age, what would it be?

193

If you had to declare a new regional or national holiday in honor of somebody famous, whom would you choose?

194

If you could take a personal tour of any famous person's home, whose home would you choose?

195

What is one TV show or movie that almost everyone else has seen that you've *never* seen?

If any one presidential nominee that lost could have won, whom would you want it to have been?

"I'd love to have my own personal _____." How would you fill in the blank?

If you could be a part of any tournament in the world, what tournament would you choose? (Assume that you have the ability to compete at the appropriate level.)

199

If you could change the ending to any movie you've ever seen, what movie would it be and how would you alter the way it ends?

200

If you could have played the leading role in any movie, what movie would you have starred in?

201

If you were invited to be the main guest on the show "This Is Your Life," what three people from your past can you imagine making a surprise visit during the show?

202

If you could "uninvent" any past invention, which one would it be? (Consider all the ramifications of eliminating this invention.)

If an architect or engineer offered to build you anything you wanted free of charge—anything at all—what would you tell them to build for you?

204

What is the best piece of advice you've ever received?

205

If you could play any position in any professional sport, which position in which sport would you choose?

206

What is the most memorable weekend you've ever experienced?

207

If you could bring back any tradition that seems to have faded into the past, what tradition would you bring back?

If you could be holding any object right now—any object in the world—what would you want in your grasp?

209

If you could have anyone else's smile, whose smile would you want?

210

Assume that you are an artist and have been asked to paint a beautiful picture for a highly respected gallery. They've given you only one stipulation: A big, beautiful moon must somehow be incorporated into the painting. Since the rest of the work has been left to your creativity, what scene would the moon be looking down upon?

211

If you were a tree, what would be your favorite month of the year?

212

Suppose that you owned a jukebox but it could only be loaded one time and with only three songs. Since you'll be hearing these songs over and over and over again, you'll want to choose the records carefully; which three songs would you pick?

What is one event that many people consider entertaining that you personally would have a very difficult time sitting through from beginning to end?

If you could have grown up in any town or city other than the one in which you really did, what location would you choose?

To the best of your knowledge, what is the fastest speed you've ever personally driven a vehicle?

216

How much money would you be willing to pay right now for the opportunity to have dinner tomorrow night with any superstar of your choice?

217

If you could help resolve any national or international dispute in the world right now, which one would it be?

218

In your opinion, what is the most thrilling type of finish in all of sports?

219

If you could own any machine in the world, what machine would you want?

220

If you were a contestant on a trivia-style game show, what category would you most want to see displayed when it came down to the million-dollar question?

221

If you had to spend the next ten years of your life living through any past decade in history, what decade would you choose? (Assume that you will enter the decade of your choice at your current age.)

Assume that you have to spend six months in total seclusion, in a room about the size of a one-car garage. You will not be allowed any visitors during these months, but you may take with you any three objects of your choice, provided you can carry them in your arms when you enter the room. Food, drink, and clothing will be provided for you daily. What three objects would you bring along?

What is something that has not yet been invented that you think *should* be invented?

What invention or discovery do you suppose probably came as the greatest shock to the people living in the era in which that invention or discovery was made?

If you could completely eliminate one genre of music, which type would you eliminate?

226

What is something you enjoy doing that would probably surprise many of the people who think they know you well?

227

On a scale of one to ten (with one being not at all and ten being very much so), how superstitious are you?

228

If you were attending a rodeo, what event would you want to see most of all?

229

What creature, more than any other, would have you scared stiff if it were loose in your home?

230

Whose autobiography, one that you haven't read to this point, would you be most interested in perusing?

231

Aside from any family occurrence (marriage, birth of a child, etc.), what singular event would you consider to be the highlight of your life thus far?

232

If you could set any famous document or speech to music, which one would you choose?

233

If you could hear a debate between any two famous people, living or deceased, who hold opposing viewpoints, whom would you want to hear and what would be the topic of their debate?

234

If you were asked to design a float for the New Year's Day Tournament of Roses Parade, what would make your float unique?

What is the most outrageous thing that has ever happened to you or in which you have ever been involved?

When was the last time you laughed so hard that you cried?

If you could greatly enhance any one of your five senses, which one would you choose?

238

If you could learn one trade secret from any leading figure in his or her respective field, what piece of information would you want disclosed and whom would you ask? (Assume that you would be given an honest answer.)

239

What age, when you turned it, was the most difficult for you to accept?

240

Which of your birthdays did you anticipate with the greatest enthusiasm?

241

If your doorbell could chime the opening notes of any famous song whenever someone came to your door, what recognizable notes would arriving guests hear?

A laughing baby, the song of a robin, the crashing of waves…If you had to ascribe a sound to the word "hope," what sound would you give it?

243

If you could safely visit one of the other planets—Mercury, Venus, Mars, Jupiter, Saturn, Uranus, Neptune, or Pluto—which one would you choose? (Note: The planets are listed here in order of shortest to longest distance from the sun.)

244

In terms of the actual time (e.g., five P.M.), what is generally your favorite time of the day?

245

If you could start a new dance craze, what would it be called and how might it be performed?

246

What is your all-time favorite line from a big-screen movie? (Example: Arnold Schwarzenegger's "I'll be back!")

247

If you could take one ethnic custom that is popular in another country and popularize it in our own culture, which custom would you pick?

248

It has long been said that one way you can help yourself to fall asleep is by counting sheep. If this technique of counting something could help *you* more easily get to sleep, what would you count in your mind each night as you lay in bed?

249

When you meet someone for the first time, what particular fact about them are you most interested in learning as quickly as possible?

If you came into enough money so that you never had to work another day in your life, what do you think you would typically do to stay busy or keep your mind occupied?

251

If you could be instantly received as a member of any club, group, or organization in the world, which one would you choose?

252

What is one book that you have read that you would love to see made into a movie?

253

Aside from anything romantic, if any particular moment in your life could have lasted five minutes longer, what moment would you want it to have been?

254

If you could be a contestant on any TV game show, past or present, which show would you pick?

255

If you had the talent and were given the chance to play in the band of any singer or musical group, past or present, whose band would you choose?

256

Suppose that at the snap of your fingers, any one thing in your home would be instantly cleaned. What would you want it to be?

If you were in charge of creating and naming a new shade of lipstick for a cosmetics company, what creative name would you give the new color?

If a movie were being made about your life and you could choose any Hollywood actor to play you in the film, whom would you choose?

259

If you were to die tomorrow, what would you want people to remember you for most of all?

260

If you were given the flat rooftop of a tall city building to develop however you chose, what would you create on your island in the sky?

If you could instantly free your mind forever of something that causes you stress in life, what worry would you get rid of?

262

What is the c-c-c-coldest that you have ever been in your life?

263

If you could guarantee the preservation of any one piece of land—large or small—for all time, what land would you choose?

264

If you could create an all-new piece of equipment for a playground, what would it be?

265

If you had to rename the street that you live on, what would you name it?

266

If you could give your current job a new title, one that would make your job seem far more exciting or important than it actually is, what would you choose as your new title?

267

What is one sports record that you're quite certain will not be broken during your lifetime?

268

What is your favorite instrument to hear when it is played by a professional musician?

269

If you were given the opportunity to be an apprentice to any person, living or deceased, from whom would you want to learn?

270

If you could have been the real-life owner of any TV or movie animal, which one would you choose?

271

Who is the most famous person you've ever met face-to-face?

272

What is one thing you thoroughly enjoy doing that a large percentage of people would probably consider trite and boring at best?

273

Although being lost is rarely enjoyable, consider the following: If you had to be lost somewhere, where would it be the most fun?

274

Which particular facial feature of yours do you personally admire the most?

If you were making a list of the five things that make you happiest in life, what five things would you write down?

If you could receive one free hour-long lesson in anything you want, what type of lesson would you request?

277

On a scale of one to ten (with one being not at all and ten being very much so), how patriotic do you think you are?

278

If you had to spend one entire summer working at one of our national parks or historic sites, which one would you choose?

If you had to update (that is, modernize) the plot in a book that is considered a classic, what book would you choose and how would the plot be changed so that it is consistent with today's world?

280

Besides the standards—books, magazines, and TV—what is one thing that you would like to see placed in every waiting room in the country?

281

If you could receive free, unlimited airline flights from your nearest airport to any one destination in the world, to what place would you be frequently flying?

Aside from a member of your own family, what person do you more or less hold up as your role model in life?

283

If you were in charge of choosing the site for the next Winter Olympic Games, what city and country would you choose?

284

What is the worst traffic jam you have ever been caught in?

285

If you could listen to the music of only one composer for the rest of your life, which composer would you choose?

What is the most exciting thing that you've done during the last twelve months?

If you had to enter a talent competition tomorrow, what would you more than likely do on stage?

288

If you had to come up with something that would take the place of a wedding band to serve as an object of union and commitment for marriage, what would you choose?

289

Throughout our history, it has been different things: a plot of land, a family car, a beautiful home. . . . Fifty years from now, what do you think will be the "Great American Dream"?

Suppose that you are an author who has to create a fictional town—like Garrison Keillor did with Lake Wobegon. What would you name your town, where would it be located, and what would be the distinguishing characteristics of the town and its people?

If you had to be of a different ethnic origin than you actually are, to which heritage would you most like to belong?

292

If you could build your home out of any structure or object besides a traditional house, what structure would serve as the framework for your home? (Example: A barn.)

293

If you had to take the year-round climate from any other part of the country and permanently have it in *your* part of the country, what region's climate would you choose?

Suppose that income taxes still had to be paid, but instead of going to the government, your tax dollars would go to any one cause or charity of your choice. Where would you want your money to go?

If you had to design a new place of worship that is, architecturally, radically different from the norm, how would you design it?

296

If you were completely deaf but could somehow hear one particular sound whenever you were within earshot of it, what sound would you choose?

297

If you could become fully enlightened instantly on any one subject, which subject would you choose?

298

If you could synchronize anything at all to music for an entertaining show, what would it be?

299

In your opinion, what flavor of ice cream would best describe your disposition?

300

If you could decorate anything at all with hundreds of thousands of tiny twinkling lights, what would you want to light up?

301

Other than money, if you could instantly have twice as much of something as you currently have, what would you want to double? (Your choice can be either tangible or intangible.)

302

Suppose that five thousand years from now, an archaeologist was digging around the ruins of the lost civilization of the United States. If the only thing that he could uncover was a perfectly preserved common penny, what are some things he would learn about our culture from simply studying that coin?

What is the most creative way you can think of to use the questions in this book?

About the Authors

The Question Guys™, **Bret Nicholaus** and **Paul Lowrie**, are full-time writers, product developers, and public speakers. Their degrees are in public relations and marketing, respectively. They have written twelve books and have created a syndicated radio show and two board games. Nicholaus lives in the Chicago area; Lowrie resides in South Dakota.

Schools, libraries, and organizations: If you are interested in booking **Bret** and **Paul** for an event, please write to them at the following address. They will get back to you within two weeks.

Bret Nicholaus and
Paul Lowrie
P.O. Box 340
Yankton, South Dakota
57078

The Question Guys™ would like to thank and acknowledge the following adults, children, and groups that helped them brainstorm ideas for some of the questions that appear in this book. Their contributions are greatly appreciated.

Employees of the Barnes & Noble Bookstore,
Wheaton, Illinois:

Linda Wallace

Jennifer Amaranth

Rachael Vaughan

Lynn Nulicek

John Gombotz

Patrick Schneider

Barnes & Noble Customers:

Lisa Gudmundson

Meghan Kennedy

Michael Smith

Connor and Kelsey Byrne

Laura Tober

Patrick Carr

Brooke Schoen

Members of Grace Lutheran Church,
LaGrange, Illinois:

Pastor Matthew Marohl

Joel Strom

Dave and Missy Kopp

Joyce Nemec

Karen Collins

Dorothy Johnson

Bob and Lois Angstadt

Joanne Hill

Mary Sherry

Ruth Chilstrom

Vickie Miller

Lorrie Nicholaus

Sara Marohl

George and Sue Davis

Alice Ewert

Sue Collins

Ann Johnson

Violet Tjernberg

Janet Angstadt

Elaine Hooven

Anne Chilstrom

Lynne Hurdle

Christina Nicholaus

Close Friends of Grace Church:

Randy Bray   Irene Sienas

**Awana Club of
the Wheaton Evangelical Free Church:**

Sally Clendening   Amy Solawa
Cara Solawa   Kara Franklin
Mary Alice Ryan   Cory Ostermann
Brandon Bocianski   Miles Bocianski
Hannah Gurunian   Liyah Gurunian

Wheaton Moms and Kids:

Cathy Smith   Andrew Smith
Darcy Holland   Monica Holland
Jill Stoffels   Jenny Stoffels
Thomas Stoffels   Gwen Johnson
Alex Johnson   Barbara Redderoth
Alexandra Redderoth   Marcy Watson
Colin Watson   Haley Watson

**Scouts from Longfellow Elementary School,
Wheaton, Illinois:**

Jordan Ellerman   Joseph Skager
Ben Haist

Boy Scout Troop 374 from Pleasant Hill School, Wheaton, Illinois:

Kasey Jedanchowski
Zackary Schulz
Alexandra DePino

Kevin Jedanchowski
David DePino
Brian Buri

Third Grade Classes, Emerson School, Wheaton, Illinois:

Mrs. Simcox and Mrs. Handbury (Teachers)

Dave Donndelinger
Zach Eastman
Mike Garrett
Jay Hindersman
Jocelyn Krisch
Katie McGinnis
Dan Nottke
Alex Remmel
Amanda Stocchero
Alex Krupnik
Anya Krenicki
Brandon Mueller
Dana Cortino
Gabe Donndelinger
Jeff Nankervis
Kyle Duhig
Rachael Bradley
Tony Montinola
Victoria Robinson

Frankie Duarte
Randal Ellison
George Hernandez
Matthew Impola
Hayley Maher
Valerie Medina
Amber Reese
Heather Ronaldson
Roger Underwood
Andrew Byerly
Ariel Burke
Brandon Rorer
Deidra Nelson
Haley Watson
Jonathan Frano
Liam Canavan
Stephanie Janda
Travis Steele

Karen Felker and Erin Breidenbaugh (Teachers)

Jack DeAno

Eric Ebbert

Allison Fountain

Michael Hible

Timmy Krueger

Keith Maltese

April Perez

Dominick Schmit

Gaetano Tangorra

Susanna Walsh

Robert Donaldson

Jessica Fenton

Ross Heise

Bethany Holaway

Zachary Malone

Parth Patel

Myles Philipp

Jill Siar

Berthane Tebarek

Nancy Young Elementary School Student Council:

Ms. Tracy Dixon and Mrs. Laura Nylen (Faculty)

Shawn Harris

Jessica Hinkemeyer

April Dyson

Angela Grabski

Kurt Benes

Kaitlin Knaszak

Adam McParlane

Drew Nolan

Kara Stevenson

Tattiana Rendon

Kylee Alexander

Christina Lopez

Katharine Chang

LeShayna Bell

Brittany Potts

Marlette Grimes

Aaron Westbrook

Julie Bandas

Megan Price

Katie Larsen

Ken Dickenscheidt

Analisa Haroldsen

Joey Vacca

Valerie Vasseur

Justin Thompson

Cassie Culler

Mari Muro

**Spring Brook Elementary School,
Naperville, Illinois**

Faculty Members:

Mr. Carl Pinnow

Mrs. Jeanine Bushias

Mrs. Nita Hinshaw

Parents of Students:

Mrs. Carol Jackson

Mrs. Maureen Klus

Mrs. Chris Barry

Mrs. Leslie Hammersmark

Third Grade:

Heather Herzog

Phillip Kuo

Alex Lincoln

Andrew Stirk

Sean Hayward

Grace Heimert

Geoff Rafferty

Mark Jackson

Jackie Lai

Kevin Overholt

Madeline Acquqviva

Grant Hedrick

Nate Kaplan

Jonathan Tomberlin

Fourth Grade:

Courtney Anderson

Swati Bhagavatula

Jeremy Lai

Lindsey Prozorovsky

P.J. Barry

Rose Branda

Andrew Banko

Lauren Hock

Joseph Ou

Adam Stack

David Bollweg

Stephanie Caballero

Billy LaRue
Jackie Saumweber
Edward Cheng
Hannah Kim
Brian Pastiak
Ashwin Torke

Kevin Liu
Claire Branda
Beth Goldberg
Brandon Lien
Casey Perkins

Fifth Grade:

Steven Hammersmark
Bernard Hsu
Karen Schmitz
Chris MacGill
Kelsey Porecca
Katie Stirk
John Wills
Matt Long
Duke Shelley
Katherine Soltys
Ryan Walsh

Maggie Hornick
Carolyn Rendos
Daniel Shearer
Brynne Nicolsen
Dean Sangalis
Ana Werkowski
Jimmy Klus
Jocelyn Ou
Amy Sneed
Katie Spencer

Tuesday Night Faculty Group:

Ms. Ann Erickson
Miss Michelle Footer

Mrs. Cindy Brown
Miss Nicole Zaccaria

Barnes & Noble
Community Relations Managers:
Bill Ezrin, Wheaton Barnes & Noble
Jo Ellen Mauer, Naperville Barnes & Noble